huh
huh huh

quaack

flutter
flitter

eeeeeeeeeeeeeeeeeeeeeeeeeeeeee

WHOOSH

R

whee-weeee

wark   wark
wark   wark
wark   wark

WHOOP

MMMOO

CROAK

T-RUM

H

zzzzzzzzzzzzzzzzzzzz

sniff

To Matthew James

First U.S. edition 1995

Simon & Schuster Books for Young Readers
An imprint of Simon & Schuster Children's Publishing Division
Simon & Schuster Macmillan
1230 Avenue of the Americas
New York, New York 10020

SIMON & SCHUSTER BOOKS FOR YOUNG READERS
is a trademark of Simon & Schuster.

First published in Great Britain in 1995
by Frances Lincoln Limited, 4 Torriano Mews
Torriano Avenue, London NW5 2RZ

Thanks to Andrew Hallsworth of London Zoo for advice
on the animal noises.
Animal noises designed and hand lettered by Jemima Lumley.

Printed and bound in Singapore

10 9 8 7 6 5 4 3 2 1

Library of Congress Cataloging-in-Publication Data
Wood, Jakki.
    Animal hullabaloo : a wildlife noisy book / Jakki Wood. – 1st
U.S. ed.
    p.   cm.
ISBN 0-689-80301-X
    1. Animal sounds—Juvenile literature. [1. Animal sounds.]
I. Title.
QL765.W65 1995
591.59–dc20   94-35206

JAKKI WOOD'S
ANIMAL
HULLABALOO
A wildlife noisy book

SIMON & SCHUSTER BOOKS FOR YOUNG READERS

crow

cuckoo

dragonfly

hen

cow

goose

chicks

sheep

pig

cockerel

mole

duck

donkey

goat

turkey

elephant

lion

hippopotamus

saddle-bill stork

turaco

tree frog

seagull

snake

crocodile

rhinoceros

seal

gnat

owl

kookaburra

bat

moth

wolf

bear

mountain lion

marmot

dingo